Dividend Income
Growing Wealth through Smart Stock Market Investments

Table of Contents

Chapter 1. Introduction

Discover the forgotten secret of the investing world with our Special Report on "Dividend Income: Growing Wealth through Smart Stock Market Investments". Untangle the complexities of the stock market and take a deep, insightful plunge into the alluring world of dividends. If you're an investor seeking stable returns and financial independence, or simply curious about the possibilities out there, this report is an absolute must-read. We'll traverse the landscapes of investment strategies together, bringing the seemingly elusive topic of dividends down to earth. Find out how the often overlooked strength of dividends could be your ticket to building enduring wealth, all in a language as clear as your morning coffee. Don't miss out on this golden opportunity to turn your dreams into reality. Intrigued? Adventurous? Let's dive in!

Chapter 2. Unveiling the Power of Dividends

Let's start our journey by stepping back into the annals of financial history and first understanding what dividends are and why they came into existence.

2.1. From the Beginning

The word 'Dividend' comes from the Latin word 'Dividendum' which means 'thing to be divided'. In the simplest of terms, dividends are portions of a company's profit, distributed to its shareholders in line with their shareholding percentage. Essentially, when a company decides to share its net earnings with investors, it's often done in the form of dividends. However, it's worth noting that not all companies choose to do so.

Dividends first became a common practice among businesses in the late 19th and early 20th centuries. Before this, companies mostly retained their earnings to finance future growth. But as corporations matured and began generating consistent profits, they started returning part of those profits to shareholders as a means of attracting more investors. This tradition of sharing profits has continued right through to the modern era.

2.2. Why do Companies Pay Dividends?

You may wonder why a company would choose to pay dividends, thereby reducing the amount of profit it can reinvest in its own growth. The reasons vary widely depending on the company's stage of development, its industry, and its existing capital structure.

Established companies in mature industries - think utilities, consumer staples, and telecommunications - often have fewer opportunities for further reinvestment and are more likely to pay out dividends.

Sharing dividends can signal to the market that the company has a strong, predictable cash flow and is confident in its future earnings prospects. This practice can attract long-term, buy-and-hold investors.

2.3. Dividend Policies and Determinants

The specifics of a company's dividend policy can tell you a lot about the company. Factors that may influence the policy include profitability, debt levels, and investment opportunities. Companies may opt for various kinds of policies - a constant dividend per share policy, constant payout ratio policy, or a residual dividend policy where the dividend is based on earnings after planned capital expenditures and working capital needs.

Moreover, a company's Board of Directors determines the actual timing and amount of dividends. While certain legalities and contractual obligations limit their discretion, they ultimately decide whether to pay dividends, how much, and when.

2.4. How Does This Benefit You?

Dividends, especially those that are consistently growing, can provide an excellent supplement to the returns gained from capital appreciation. For long-term investors, dividends can be a particularly attractive feature for several reasons.

1. Income Source: Dividends provide a regular stream of income on top of any gains from the increase in stock price. This can be

especially beneficial for those nearing retirement or those who prefer a more passive income stream.

2. Mitigation of Market Risks: Dividends can serve as a cushion during periods of market uncertainty or downturns. Even when the stock price is not performing well, dividends can provide some level of returns.

3. Reinvestment Opportunities: Dividends can also be reinvested through a Dividend Reinvestment Plan (DRIP). This process automatically uses the dividends to buy more shares of the company, offering a way to grow your investment incrementally over time.

2.5. Dividend Yield and Dividend Growth

The dividend yield is a financial ratio that indicates how much a company pays out in dividends each year relative to its share price. It's often expressed as a percentage. A high dividend yield can be an indication of a good income-generating stock, but it's also essential to look at the overall health of the company.

On the other hand, dividend growth demonstrates how a company's dividend payment has grown over an extended period. Consistent dividend growth can be a signal of a financially health company with strong performance and profitability prospects.

2.6. Spotting Quality Dividend Stocks

While dividends can be attractive, it's essential to look beyond just the yield. A high dividend yield might be a result of a drastically falling stock price. Therefore, examine other fundamental aspects of the company, including earnings stability, debt levels, and future growth prospects.

Further, look at the company's history of dividend payments. Have they consistently paid dividends? Have they regularly increased their dividend payout? Consistency is typically a good indicator of a company's commitment to returning profits to shareholders.

2.7. Incorporating Dividends in your Investment Strategy

Every investor has unique financial needs, risk profiles, and investment goals. Therefore, the role of dividends in an investment strategy will vary from investor to investor. However, for those who appreciate a stable income stream and a level of insulation against market downturns, incorporating dividends might prove to be a smart move.

In summary, dividends represent a significant part of a company's story and can serve as a powerful tool in investment strategies when understood and used appropriately. With proper knowledge and due diligence, investors can exploit this often overlooked power of dividends to drive their investment growth and income. Stay tuned as we continue to uncover more about dividends in the subsequent chapters.

Chapter 3. Understanding Investments: Stocks and Dividends

When conversing about investments in the financial sphere, two prominent assets invariably stand out: stocks and dividends. In our journey today, we will lift the veil surrounding these concepts, dispel the prevailing myths about their complexity, and illuminate how these powerful tools can assist in growing and safeguarding wealth.

3.1. An Introduction to Stocks

Before journeying into the depths of dividends, we must first understand their foundation – stocks. Stocks, also referred to as shares or equities, represent a unit of ownership in a corporation. When an investor purchases a share in a company, they effectively purchase a chunk of that company's assets and earnings.

The appeal of investing in stocks over a long-term horizon is that it allows shareholders to partake in the company's success through an increase in market value. As a company flourishes, the demand for its stock tends to grow, causing its share price to rise. It's worth noting, however, that the opposite can also be true. If the company underperforms or faces bankruptcy, the share price can drop, resulting in potential losses for investors.

The stock market, where these transactions occur, is a vast, dynamic entity. Fortunately, elaborate knowledge of its every nook and cranny is not requisite. The key lies in understanding the foundational elements and strategizing intelligently.

3.2. Classifications of Stocks

Different flavors of stocks appeal to distinct kinds of investors, based on their financial goals, risk tolerance and investment horizon. Primarily, stocks are categorized into two types: common and preferred.

Common stocks typically grant shareholders the right to vote at company meetings and receive dividends, which is a slice of company earnings usually paid out to shareholders. However, in a liquidation scenario, common stockholders stand last in line to receive any leftover assets, following creditors and preferred stockholders.

On the other hand, preferred stocks entitle their holders to a fixed dividend, distributed before any dividends to common stockholders. While they lack the voting rights, they carry less risk, as in case of liquidation, they get paid before the common stockholders.

3.3. Entering the Dividend Realm

Dividends are payments made by a corporation to its shareholder members. They are a portion of earnings that the company returns to its shareholders. Paying dividends does not mean a company is in good financial health, but it is often interpreted as a good financial sign because it shows that the company has a stable cash flow.

Knowing when a company decides to pay dividends is crucial. This usually happens in a company's maturity stage, when the rate of growth is slowing down and substantial funds are no longer necessary for reinvesting to drive further growth.

3.4. Types of Dividends

Understanding the varying types of dividends is integral to pursuing a dividend-focused investment strategy. Primarily, dividends are categorized into two major types: cash and stock dividends.

Cash dividends are the most prevalent type, distributed as a monetary payment. The beauty of cash dividends resides in the flexibility they offer. The investor can choose to reinvest the dividend, spend it, or even add it to the stack of savings.

Stock dividends, conversely, involve the distribution of additional stocks to the shareholders proportional to their existing holdings. This allows investors to maintain their proportional ownership in the company, while the capital remains inside the corporation.

3.5. The Power of Dividend Investing

Dividend-focused investing can act as a sustainable wealth-building approach for a myriad of reasons. Firstly, they provide a stable income stream. This becomes particularly important during financial downturns, where capital gains can be far from guaranteed. This aspect can make a dividend-focused approach especially appealing for retirees or those nearing retirement.

Moreover, the regular payment of dividends can be seen as a reflection of a company's financial health and stability. Companies with a consistent dividend payment history are often financially mature, well-established entities with regular cash flows.

The ability to reinvest dividends through a dividend reinvestment plan (DRIP) is another viable proposition. By automatically reinvesting dividends into more shares, you can catalyze the process of compound growth, an investment phenomenon where earnings begin to generate their own earnings over time.

Despite its enticing virtues, dividend investing is not without risks.

The possibility of companies slashing their dividends or the presence of high dividend yields to mask underlying issues are potential caveats investors must be aware of.

3.6. Wielding Dividends for Wealth Management

By balancing the pursuit of dividend income with a broader investment strategy that encompasses capital appreciation, investors can work towards creating a robust portfolio that stands the test of time. Eventually, understanding the moving parts of stocks and dividends, how they intertwine, and their impacts on your financial goals can be your linchpin for achieving financial independence.

In essence, stocks and dividends are powerful tools in the investing arsenal, and understanding them paves the way for a fruitful journey in the world of investments. With this foundational knowledge, you are armed and ready to delve further into the specific strategies that utilize dividends to create a river of potential income. Knowledge is indeed power when it comes to the investing world. Whether you are just starting your journey or are a seasoned investor, understanding the intricate dance between stocks and dividends is a vital stepping stone on your path to financial freedom.

Chapter 4. Decoding Dividend Stocks: What Makes Them Special?

Investing in the stock market can be an overwhelming experience, particularly for novices unaware of the various strategies to employ and securities to choose from. Amid the legion of options available, one investment method has steadily beaten the odds for generations, namely investing in dividend stocks. As the cornerstone of a balanced investment portfolio, understanding the peculiarities of dividend stocks can provide significant momentum towards achieving financial independence.

4.1. What Are Dividend Stocks?

Dividend stocks are shares of publicly traded companies that distribute a portion of their earnings back to shareholders. Companies distribute these earnings, known as dividends, typically on a quarterly basis, either in the form of cash or additional shares. The size of a dividend is determined by the company's board of directors and is normally expressed as a percentage of the current share price, also known as the dividend yield.

Dividend stocks come from companies that usually have a long history of financial stability and steady profits. They belong to the mature phase of their business lifecycle, possessing a lower risk profile compared to high-growth startups. Industries such as utilities, consumer goods, and real estate often house dividend-yielding stocks.

4.2. The Lure of Dividend Paying Stocks

The true appeal of dividend stocks lies in two areas: reliability and compounding.

Reliability stems from the track record of the paying company. Established corporations with a consistent past of positive earnings are the ones that offer dividends. They demonstrate a degree of resilience against market downturns, thus providing a stable revenue stream to investors.

The magic of compounding, the process where earnings are reinvested to generate their own earnings, further magnifies the appeal of dividend stocks. Reinvesting dividends results in more shares, which in turn produce more dividends, thus initiating a virtuous cycle of compounding returns.

4.3. Evaluating Dividend Stocks: Key Parameters

Investing in dividend stocks is not as simple as picking the stock with the highest yield. Several key parameters should be considered for a holistic evaluation.

1. Dividend Yield: This is the annual dividend divided by the stock's current market price. A good yield is usually around 2-6%.

2. Payout Ratio: It's calculated as the annual dividend per share divided by earnings per share. A lower payout ratio suggests that the company can comfortably afford its dividend payments.

3. Dividend Growth: Firms that steadily increase their dividends provide an inflation-protected income stream.

4. Revenue and Earnings Stability: Companies with stable earnings

are more likely to deliver consistent dividends.

5. Debt-To-Equity Ratio: Companies with low debt can withstand economic downturns without drastic dividend cuts.

4.4. Choosing the Right Dividend Stocks

Before deciding to invest in a dividend stock, ensure it fits your overall investment strategy and risk tolerance. For investors aiming for long-term growth and financial security, stocks paying consistent and increasing dividends are a fitting choice.

Investors should also balance their portfolio by including a diverse range of dividend stocks from various economic sectors. This diversification helps mitigate industry-specific risks that may jeopardize dividend payouts. Services of professional financial advisors or adoption of Dividend Reinvestment Plans (DRIPs) can simplify this process.

Dividend investing is not a get-rich-quick scheme. The real benefit comes in the long run by way of stable income and compounding. Therefore, patience and discipline are critical for success in this strategy.

In conclusion, the often overlooked allure of dividend stocks lies in their potential for steady income and exponential growth via compounding. By understanding their intricacies and selecting wisely, investors can unlock a powerful tool for wealth generation. This knowledge, coupled with patience and a conservative approach, can help turn the tide in favor of every investor, from the novice to the seasoned. The beauty of dividend stocks transcends the simple act of investing, opening doors to financial independence and stability.

Chapter 5. The Art of Identifying High-Yield Dividend Stocks

Investing in high-yield dividend stocks is far from a random process. It requires keen understanding, methodical planning, and a touch of shrewd diligence. This journey may seem long, but the outcome is well worth the effort.

5.1. Understanding Dividends

A dividend is the distribution of a portion of a company's profits to its shareholders. These dividends are typically paid in cash, but can also be in the form of additional shares of stock. Companies that consistently provide dividends are generally stable and profitable, making them attractive for investors looking for predictable returns.

Dividend yield is one of the key factors that investors look at when choosing dividend stocks. It is calculated by dividing the annual dividend payment by the market price per share of the company's stock. For example, if a company pays an annual dividend of $2 per share, and the current stock price is $50, the dividend yield would be 4%.

The higher the dividend yield, the better the return on investment. However, an abnormally high yield could be a red flag. These companies might not be able to maintain their high dividend payments, which could lead to disappointment for investors.

5.2. The Importance of Dividend History

A company's dividend history is often an accurate indicator of its financial health. Stable or increasing dividends over time signal a company's consistent profitability. Investors need to be wary of companies which have a history of erratic dividend payment.

For instance, if a company has maintained or increased its dividends over a period of ten years, it's a good indication of healthy cash flow and prudent financial management. But if dividends fluctuate wildly or have been cut in the past, it signifies potential instability.

5.3. Earnings and Payout Ratio

Two more crucial factors in identifying high-yield dividend stocks are earnings and payout ratio. Company's earnings should steadily grow over time. If earnings are highly inconsistent, it may affect the company's ability to provide dividends consistently.

The payout ratio - expressed as a percentage - shows the portion of earnings a company uses to pay dividends to shareholders. A lower payout ratio implies that a company retains more profit for growth, while a higher ratio could indicate that the company is returning more to shareholders. Generally, a payout ratio of less than 60% is considered healthy.

5.4. Debt to Equity Ratio

It's also important to consider a company's debt to equity ratio. This measures the financial leverage of a company, comparing its total liabilities to shareholders' equity. A lower ratio usually indicates a relatively less risky investment. Companies with high debt levels are more vulnerable during economic downturns and could potentially cut dividends.

5.5. Sector and Industry Trends

Different sectors and industries have varied inclinations towards dividends. Certain sectors, like utilities, real estate investment trusts (REITs) and consumer staples tend to be high-yielding due to their reliable income streams and profitability. Understanding these trends can help investors focus their efforts.

5.6. The Significance of Dividend Sustainability

Even though a stock may have a high yield, it doesn't necessarily mean it's a good investment. The ability of a company to sustain its dividend payments is crucial. It depends on factors such as net income, free cash flow, and corporate policies.

For instance, if a company has a high dividend yield but low earnings, it might not manage to sustain the dividend payout. Similarly, a company might choose to direct its income to other areas like debt repayment, reinvestments, or acquisitions, affecting its dividend payment in the process.

5.7. Decoding the Dividend Trap

High dividend yields can sometimes act as a trap, often known as a "dividend trap". These are situations when a stock's dividend yield is high only because the stock's price is falling faster than dividends are being cut. They are dangerous because they lure investors with the promise of high returns only to result in capital losses.

Under these circumstances, it's key to look at the overall performance of the company and the reason behind the falling share prices. A sudden plunge coupled with a high yield could be a significant warning sign.

5.8. Final Thoughts

In conclusion, identifying high-yield dividend stocks is not simply a case of picking the stocks with the highest yields. It's about thorough research, studying company fundamentals, understanding the market environment, sector trends, and an array of financial indicators. Economical diligence and patience are the true companions of any successful dividend investor. Regard investing as a continual learning process, and the path of dividends can become a journey of substantial wealth creation.

Chapter 6. Investment Strategies: The Path to Accumulating Dividend Wealth

Let's begin by grasping an understanding of investment strategies, specifically how they relate to dividend stocks. Investment strategies, in its broadest terms, encompasses your plan of action designed to help you achieve your long-term financial goal. They are primarily defined by your personal financial goals, risk tolerance, and investment time frame. When it comes to investing in dividend-paying stocks, these strategies can vastly influence the kind of returns you obtain.

6.1. Understanding Dividend Stocks

Dividend stocks represent companies that distribute a portion of their earnings back to the shareholders. These distributions, better known as dividends, provide a continual income stream, making these stocks an attractive investment choice. But why should you consider diving into the world of dividends? Stocks that pay dividends are typically companies that have stable and established business models, often translating to lower investment risk compared to companies that don't pay dividends to their shareholders.

6.2. Dividend Stocks - Choosing Quality over Quantity

When investing in dividend stocks, it's important to note that a higher yield doesn't always entail a better investment. In some cases, a company with a high dividend yield may be struggling with its finances and is desperate to attract investors. Thus, rather than just looking at the dividend yield, also look at other important metrics such as the payout ratio and the company's history of dividend increases. A lower payout ratio could mean that the company is retaining more profits for growth, and a history of regular dividend increases could indicate a company's stability.

6.3. Dividend Reinvestment Plan and Direct Stock Purchase Plan

Reinvesting dividends through a Dividend Reinvestment Plan (DRIP) or a Direct Stock Purchase Plan (DSPP) is a powerful way to accumulate wealth. Instead of receiving dividends in cash, your dividends are automatically used to buy more shares of the company. This allows your investment to compound over time, resulting in potentially significant growth of your initial investment.

6.4. Constructing a Dividend Portfolio

Now, let's focus on building a bona fide dividend portfolio. A well-rounded portfolio doesn't have all its assets tied to a single stock or sector. It's diversified and has a fine balance between High-Dividend Yield stocks and Dividend Growth stocks.

High-Dividend Yield Stocks: These stocks typically attract investors seeking steady income. However, the trade-off can often be slower company growth and higher risk.

Dividend Growth Stocks: These are stocks with a track record of regularly increasing their dividends. The dividend increase is often a strong signal that the company's financial health is sound.

To balance your portfolio, invest in a mix of the two. This balancing act mitigates the potential risks while aiming for steady returns.

6.5. Investing in Dividend ETFs

Another way to gain exposure to dividends is through ETFs or Dividend Exchange Traded Funds. ETFs give you the benefit of diversification as they are a basket of different securities. They can provide exposure to a specific sector, index, or type of stock. Dividend ETFs specifically focus on dividend-paying stocks, provide diversification, and spare you the hassle of picking individual stocks.

6.6. Dividend Achievers, Aristocrats, and Kings

"Dividend Achievers," "Dividend Aristocrats," and "Dividend Kings" represent groups of stocks distinguished by their impressive historical dividend performance.

Dividend Achievers are companies with a history of increasing their dividends annually for at least the past ten years.

Dividend Aristocrats have increased payments each year for the past 25 years. Notably, they're generally part of the S&P 500.

Dividend Kings are the crowned jewels, having increased their dividends annually for at least fifty years!

Choosing one or a combination of these groups can help you assemble a portfolio for consistent gains.

6.7. Final Thoughts

Investing in dividend stocks is a journey, not a destination, and it requires a keen knowledge of strategies and an understanding of market trends. It's a rewarding strategy if you have long-term perspective, are patient, and can weather fluctuations. Choose your stocks wisely, diversify your holdings, and monitor your investments regularly. Remember, it's not just about immediate returns - it's about building enduring wealth for your financial independence. So set your course, and let the magic of compound dividends power your financial journey!

Chapter 7. Long-term Vision: The Magic of Compound Interest and Dividends

In the quest for financial success, there is a cardinal rule of investing that many overlook: the power of compound interest and dividends. This might sound complex at first, but it's as simple as letting your wealth grow in silence while you engage with life's other pursuits.

7.1. Embracing the Power of Compound Interest

Compound interest is arguably one of the most powerful tools available to an investor. Simply put, it's earning interest on your interest. Sound too easy? Let's explore how powerful this seemingly simple mechanism can be.

Imagine you invest $10,000 today, and it earns an annual rate of return of 5%. At the end of the year, your investment will grow by $500 ($10,000*5%). Thereafter, you start the second year with $10,500. Now, the 5% return is applied on this new total, resulting in $525 in earnings ($10,500*5%). And this cycle continues.

Now picture this process over 20, 30, or 40 years. The amounts significantly increase to create a snowball effect, thus illustrating the magic of compound interest.

7.2. Dividends: Another Layer of Compounding

In the realm of investing, dividends provide another layer of compounding. When you own shares of a dividend-paying company, you are entitled to a portion of profits usually distributed quarterly. The most strategic investors don't spend these payments; they reinvest them to buy more shares, hence growing their future dividend income – another instance of compounding.

There's a term for this in the financial world, which is known as the "Dividend Reinvestment Plan (DRIP)". Instead of receiving dividend payments in cash, they are automatically reinvested to purchase additional shares in the company, granting investors the benefits of compounding without lifting a finger.

7.3. Choosing Dividend-Paying Companies

Not all companies award dividends to their shareholders. Many, especially those in growth phases, prefer to reinvest their profits back into their business. However, mature companies with predictable profits often distribute dividends generously. And it's these companies that a smart investor keen on leveraging the power of dividends and compound interest should target.

In choosing the right companies, consider ones with a consistent history of paying dividends and a well-articulated dividend policy. Take into account the dividend yield too, calculated by dividing annual dividends per share by price per share, as a measure of the company's value.

7.4. The Time Factor

For the magic of compound interest and dividends to work, you need one more ingredient - time. The compounding process grows your investments exponentially, and this growth takes off drastically after a few periods. So, the earlier you start investing, and the longer you keep your investments, the greater the end result will be.

7.5. Tenacious Optimism: The Investor's Compass

In this journey of building enduring wealth, there will be market downturns. These downturns often incite fear, resulting in investors selling their stocks and exiting the market. However, such actions could disrupt the magic of compounding.

Having a wise perspective during these times is crucial. Remember that market downturns are generally followed by upturns. Stay invested. Hold on to your dividend-paying stocks and continue reinvesting those dividends. Over time, your tenacious optimism will be rewarded.

Indeed, the combined impact of compound interest and dividends is a powerful strategy for long-term wealth creation. It defines a clear, path to financial independence by leveraging the time-tested principles of investing.

This makes investing exciting – it isn't simply a method to amass wealth, but more of a journey into understanding how money can work for you quietly, diligently, and continuously. You become a silent architect of your own wealth, learning about financial markets, experiencing the thrill of investing, but most importantly, understanding the power and magic of compound interest and dividends, and how these twin engines can drive your wealth to unimaginable boundaries.

By digging deeper into understanding and applying these concepts, you can navigate the tumultuous waves of investing and emerge victorious. The key is consistency and patience, armed with the powerful tools of compound interest and dividends, working harmoniously to amplify your wealth. So gear up, stay invested and see the magic unfold!

Remember, the best time to start is now. Immerse yourself in understanding these concepts and apply them diligently. In the words of Albert Einstein, "Compound interest is the eighth wonder of the world. He who understands it, earns it; he who doesn't, pays it." In the end, whether the magic of compound interest and dividends will work for you depends on your understanding and your willingness to harness their potential.

Chapter 8. Tax Implications Involving Dividend Income

Understanding the tax implications associated with dividend income is pivotal for every investor as it determines the net return on investments. While the upfront notion of receiving these periodic payouts might seem appealing, it's important to realize that these dividends aren't free money. They are, in fact, subjected to taxes and it revolves around a complex landscape of rules and regulations.

8.1. Income Taxes Based on Dividend Type

First and foremost, not all dividends are created equal. They are primarily categorized into two types: qualified dividends and non-qualified dividends, more commonly known as ordinary dividends.

Qualified dividends are those that meet specific criteria set by the IRS and are taxed at long-term capital gains tax rates, which can be considerably lower than the rates for ordinary income. On the other hand, ordinary dividends are taxed as regular income at the individual's personal income tax rate.

To qualify for the lower tax rate, a dividend must come from a U.S. company or a qualifying foreign company, the underlying shares must be held for a minimum period (more than 60 days during a 121-day period that starts 60 days before the ex-dividend date), and the dividend must not be listed by the IRS as one that does not qualify.

8.2. Foreign Dividend Taxes

An investor who holds shares in a foreign company and receives foreign dividends has to understand the additional tax implications.

These dividends from foreign corporations are often subject to a foreign tax withholding. The withholding rates can vary widely, depending on the country, and can sometimes be reclaimed or offset against U.S. taxes.

The U.S. has tax treaties with several countries to avoid double taxation. Still, one must fill out appropriate IRS forms to qualify for these tax treaty benefits.

8.3. Dividends and the Double Taxation Dilemma

A key issue which arises with dividends is the matter of 'double taxation'. Dividends are the portion of a company's profits distributed to shareholders. However, this profit is obtained after the company has paid corporate income tax. And when dividends are further taxed in the hands of the shareholders, it leads to the issue of double taxation. While some countries provide relief from such double taxation, the specifics vary based on jurisdiction and treaty agreements.

8.4. Dividend Reinvestment Plan (DRIP)

Many investors choose to reinvest their dividends back into additional shares of the same company, often using a Dividend Reinvestment Plan (DRIP). While DRIP offers the advantage of buying more shares without a commission and the benefits of compounding, it's important to understand that reinvested dividends are still subject to tax in the year they were paid. Investors are responsible for keeping records of these dividends for accurate reporting.

8.5. Taxes on Dividends in Retirement Accounts

Dividend-bearing investments in accounts like traditional IRAs or 401(k)s grow tax-deferred until withdrawal, so the tax on dividends isn't an immediate concern. However, any withdrawal from these accounts would be taxed as regular income, irrespective of their original nature.

Conversely, Roth IRAs and Roth 401(k)s grow tax-free. So, dividends reinvested in these accounts will not incur taxable income, even upon withdrawal.

8.6. Strategies to Minimize Dividend Taxes

There are several strategies for minimizing taxes on dividend income. Holding qualified dividends long enough to secure the rates for long-term capital gains can save considerably on taxes. Maximizing the use of tax-advantaged retirement accounts can also shield your dividend income from immediate taxation.

Furthermore, for investors in higher tax brackets, tax-managed funds or tax-efficient index funds may be beneficial. They're managed to minimize the distribution of taxable dividends, primarily by minimizing buying and selling within the fund.

Understanding the tax laws surrounding dividend income is as important as selecting the right investments. While tax laws might feel overwhelming, with a little patience, and perhaps some professional advice, you can navigate these laws and make the most of your dividend income.

Remember, every investment decision you make has potential tax implications. Therefore, learning and understanding these can help you be both a smarter investor and a smarter tax planner. Implementing these strategies correctly can significantly reduce your tax burden, leaving more money in your pocket- Hence, effectively improving your overall investment returns.

Chapter 9. Common Pitfalls While Investing in Dividend Stocks and How to Avoid Them

Investing in dividend stocks can be a rewarding strategy, bolstering your portfolio with regular income along with the possibility of capital appreciation. That said, numerous pitfalls can trip up both novice and seasoned investors. By recognizing these common errors, you can take steps to eliminate them from your investment approach. Our sub-chapters will delve into these pitfalls and provide strategic insights to avoid them.

9.1. Understanding Dividend Yield

The dividend yield, often portrayed as a percentage, represents the ratio of a company's annual dividends to its share price. Many investors gravitate towards stocks with high dividend yields. However, a remarkably high yield can signal danger. It could indicate that the company's share price has plummeted, possibly due to financial troubles. As such, it may not be able to sustain its dividends in the future.

To avoid this pitfall, don't simply chase high yields. Instead, examine the company's financial health, profitability, payout ratio, and dividend history. By doing so, you'll be better equipped to discern whether the yield is sustainable, or if it's a potential red flag.

9.2. Ignoring the Payout Ratio

The payout ratio, another crucial metric in dividend investing, represents the percentage of net income a company pays to shareholders as dividends. Some investors might ignore it, focusing solely on yield or growth rates. However, a high payout ratio could suggest that the company is returning more money to shareholders than it's retaining for growth. Also, a high payout can put the company in a precarious position if they hit a rough financial patch.

Avoid this pitfall by regularly examining payout ratios. Look for companies with a comfortable balance between paying dividends and retaining earnings for growth. A combination of a decent yield and a sustainable payout ratio often signifies a promising dividend stock.

9.3. Neglecting Dividend Coverage Ratio

The dividend coverage ratio, which indicates how well a company's earnings can cover its dividend payments, is often neglected. Companies with a low dividend coverage ratio may struggle to sustain their dividend payments, particularly during tough economic times.

Bypass this trap by analyzing the company's dividend coverage ratio as part of your evaluation process. The higher the dividend coverage ratio, the better a company can afford its dividends.

9.4. Overlooking Company Debt

Investing without considering a company's debt level can be disastrous. High debt can eat into profits, possibly leading to reduced dividends or, worst-case scenario, dividend cuts. Constantly monitoring a company's debt to equity ratio provides insight into its financial stability and ability to maintain its dividends.

To avoid this pitfall, beware of companies with high debt levels that could jeopardize dividend payments. A company's debt should always be manageable, even in an economic downturn.

9.5. Forgetting to Diversify

Concentrating investments in just a few dividend stocks risks exposure to sector-specific downturns or individual company issues. A well-diversified portfolio can bring stability, spread risk across multiple sectors, and provide opportunities for capital appreciation and dividends.

Escape this common trap by diversifying your investment portfolio. Investing in different sectors can help manage risk and increase opportunities for return.

9.6. Betting on Dividend Stocks for Short-Term Gains

While dividends can add an appreciable income stream to your portfolio, betting on dividend stocks for short-term gains isn't advisable. Companies with regular dividends usually offer steady, slow-growing returns over a longer period. As a rule, dividend investing is more conducive to a buy-and-hold strategy.

Avoid being ensnared by this misconception. Embrace a long-term approach through regular investing, patient waiting, and compounding dividends.

While pitfalls are inherent in investing, awareness and understanding of these common errors can greatly enhance your potential for success in dividend investing. Equip yourself with knowledge, do your due diligence, and adopt a futuristic view while investing in dividend stocks. With an informed and thoughtful approach, you stand a greater chance of achieving your financial goals through dividend investing.

Chapter 10. Case Studies: Successful Wealth Accumulation Through Dividends

As we venture into the thriving world of dividends, it is imperative to delve into the richness of historical data and real-life instances that crystallize the potential of focused dividend investing. Let us learn from the successes, strategies, and wisdom carved out by those who have already walked the path.

10.1. The Story of Tom: Slow and Steady

In the late 1980s, Tom, aged 25, started investing. He worked as a salesman, earning a modest income. He decided to allot around 15% of his monthly salary to dividend-paying stocks. Tom was drawn to companies with a track record of consistent dividend payment and growth.

Tom targeted companies such as McDonald's, Johnson & Johnson, and Proctor & Gamble, whose products he used regularly. These companies were paying dividends consistently and increasing them year by year.

Over time, Tom's portfolio swelled primarily because of two things:

1. Dividend Reinvestment: Reinvesting dividends allowed Tom to buy more stocks, augmenting his portfolio sequentially.

2. Dividend Compounding: As his reinvested dividends were used to purchase more shares, these additional shares also began

earning dividends, creating a snowball effect.

By the time Tom reached 60, he had accumulated a considerable sum that surpassed many of his contemporaries.

10.2. Strategy of Bob: Harnessing High Dividend Yields

Another case worth discussing is that of Bob, who adopted a different approach. Bob, starting his investment journey later than Tom, at age 35, sought out companies with high dividend yields. He wasn't focused solely on dividend growth; he also highly valued payout regularity.

Bob invested in some of the highest dividend-yielding companies, particularly in financial, utility, and real estate sectors. He carefully balanced his portfolio to avoid excessive concentration and saw steady returns despite the volatility of some sectors.

By strictly adhering to a diversified high-yield dividend portfolio, Bob was able to produce significant income return throughout his investing journey, allowing him to retire comfortably at the age of 65.

10.3. Kate's Philosophy: Mix of Dividend Growth and Yield

Kate, a working woman in her late twenties, was savvy with her finances early on. She understood the need for balance and pursued an investment strategy that centered around both dividend growth and high-yield stocks.

Her choice of stocks was expansive from well-established technology companies to emerging market blue-chips. This dynamism and strategic mix served her well, delivering steady returns and healthy portfolio diversification.

Not every investment Kate made was a winner, but the cumulative growth and yield of her strategic mix were powerful. By the time she was ready to retire, Kate had a substantial portfolio value that offered both stability and income for her investment goals.

These case studies underline the potential of dividend investing, both from a growth and yield perspective. The strategies differ, and so do the risk levels and returns. Yet, when done wisely—with an understanding of the companies, sectors, and overall economic trends—dividend investing can splendidly augment wealth.

10.4. Fostering a Framework for Dividend Investing Success

Each of the above stories had some commonalities.

1. The Power of Time: Having a long investment horizon is the bedrock of successful dividend investing.

2. Consistent Investing: Whether it's high-growth or high yield dividends, consistency in investment is key.

3. Portfolio Diversification: Exposure to diverse sectors and company maturity levels can provide balance and spread risk.

4. Patience: Dividends might seem puny amounts initially, but as examples demonstrate, it's their power over time that builds remarkable wealth.

As we can see, dividend investing is a strategic and calculated approach. It is not about getting rich quick. Instead, it's about harnessing the power of dividends to generate stable income and grow wealth over time. Each investor will have their unique motivations, risk tolerances, and financial objectives. It is therefore crucial that they understand and leverage the power of dividends according to their individual needs.

In the next section, we will decode, in greather detail, the mechanics and dynamics of dividends and provide tools and insights for successful dividend investing.

Chapter 11. Staying Ahead: Forecasting Future Trends in Dividend Investment

Before we delve into tracking the potentially game-changing trends of the world of dividend investing, it is essential to understand dividend investments' foundational concepts. As a refresher, dividends are payments made by a corporation to its shareholders, usually in the form of cash or additional shares. They represent a portion of corporate profits paid out to stockholders and signify a steady stream of income for investors over and above any market appreciation of their stock.

11.1. Understanding the Importance of Dividends

Dividends have held an important place in the heart of long-term investors and are considered a sign of a company's health and stability. Earning a stable dividend income can serve as a safety net in volatile times when market prices rise and fall unpredictably.

Moreover, dividends tend to rise over time, resisting effects of inflation, which can be a major boon in a long-term investment portfolio. But how exactly can you stay ahead of the curve by forecasting future trends in dividend investments?

11.2. The Art of Forecasting

Forecasting in investment terms is making educated predictions about the market's direction or about a specific stock's potential growth based on current data. It is not a guaranteed prediction, but rather a statistical probability that guides an investor's decisions.

When it comes to dividends, the art of forecasting revolves around identifying companies that could potentially increase their earnings and, hence, their dividend payments in the future. The key lies in spotting the right indicators, understanding market trends, and studying the company's history and future plans.

11.3. Spotting Financial Indicators

Financial indicators are statistical measures that provide a snapshot of a company's financial health. They can serve as an early warning signal for investors, helping to highlight whether a company is in a position to maintain or increase its dividend payments.

1. Payout Ratio: An important indicator of a company's dividend health is the payout ratio — it gives you an idea of what proportion of earnings a company is paying out as dividends. If a company has a low payout ratio, there's room for the company to increase its dividends in the future.

2. Debt-to-Equity Ratio: This ratio reflects the financial leverage of a company. A higher ratio suggests that a company relies on debt to finance its activities, which could potentially harm its ability to pay dividends in the future.

3. Retained Earnings: These represent the cumulative net income or profit of a company after it has paid out dividends to its shareholders. Companies with high retained earnings may have better chances of maintaining or increasing their dividend payments.

11.4. Understanding Market Trends

Dividend investments are in many ways a reflection of broader market trends. Anticipating these trends can provide a leading edge in forecasting dividend performance.

1. Interest Rates: If interest rates are forecasted to fall, companies have more capacity to take on manageable debt—and increased earnings could lead to increased dividends.

2. Economic Climate: A booming economy can indicate prosperous times ahead for companies and, by extension, their dividends. Keep an eye on broad economic indicators like GDP growth, unemployment rates, and consumer spending patterns.

3. Sector Trends: Specific industry sectors often move in cyclical trends—think technology, healthcare, or consumer discretionary sectors, each with their unique set of growth drivers.

11.5. Studying the Company's History and Future Plans

Doing your homework on a specific company can also reveal plenty about its potential for future dividend growth.

1. Dividend History: A strong track record of stable or increasing dividends bodes well for future payouts.

2. Future Plans: Companies often provide forward-looking statements in their quarterly and annual reports—these can provide invaluable insights into strategies that could impact profit, and consequently, dividends. Two key considerations are expansion plans (new markets, acquisitions) or operational efficiency improvements (cost-reduction strategies, streamlining).

Forecasting future trends in dividend investing may appear complex, but these tools and insights can provide the building blocks for successful, profitable investments. Remember, while forecasting is an important part of the investing process, it should be paired with thoughtful analysis and continued learning to realize your investing goals.